Rigging a Chevy into a Time Machine and Other Ways to Escape a Plague

Also by Author

Skinny
Kore Press, 2012

Rigging a Chevy into a Time Machine and Other Ways to Escape a Plague

Poems by Carolyn Hembree

2015 Trio Award Winner

Copyright © Carolyn Hembree 2016

No part of this book may be used or performed without written consent from the author, if living, except for critical articles or reviews.

Hembree, Carolyn
1st edition.

ISBN: 978-0-9965864-0-5
Library of Congress Control Number: 2015915104

Interior Layout by Lea C. Deschenes
Cover Design by Dorinda Wegener
Cover Photo of the "first observation of neutral currents in the Gargamelle bubble chamber," courtesy of
   CERN
Editing by Tayve Neese

Printed in Tennessee, USA
Trio House Press, Inc.
Ponte Vedra Beach, FL

To contact the author, send an email to tayveneese@comcast.net

for Jon

TABLE OF CONTENTS

SAFETY RESTRAINTS

3   Kill the Harbinger

6   1 1 a.m. Aubade

10   Eyecandy at 15

11   V. Cleb Has a Girl, Baptizes Her

12   His Bed Sheet in Place

13   Primer from His Forebears

INSTRUMENT CONTROL PANELS

17   Raven Spell

19   Necrology from His Forebears

21   Mama Cleb Took Up Her Homemade Torch

23   V. Cleb at 8

25   To Heavy Metal from a Boom Box

26   No Jukebox, No Payphone

27   Parable from His Forebears

WARNING LIGHTS AND GAUGES

31 Fable from His Forebears

32 Poison's Out

33 The Burnt-out Filling Station

34 Inspector in His Mint Suit

35 The Holy Ghost Might Appear

36 What Place Then for a Creator?

37 Ghosts

38 Quantum Mechanical Eyecandy

40 Devil Worshipers Say It

ROADSIDE EMERGENCIES

45 Sears Catalog Girl Grants V. Cleb the Spiritual Gifts of Flight and X-ray Vision

CUSTOMER ASSISTANCE

57 Did the Universe Have a Beginning, and If So, What Happened Before Then?

58 What Is It That Breathes Fire into the Equation and Makes a Universe to Destroy?

60 Did the Universe Have a Beginning, and If So, What Happened Before Then?

62 Why Do We Remember the Past and Not the Future?

66 Why Does the Universe Go through the Bother of Existing?

69 Notes

71 Acknowledgments

73 About the Author

Safety Restraints

Kill the Harbinger

at your screen door:
call the opossum (milk carton in hand)
like a cat, *here thing*
loose a flo
the trick's to aim high
to make that marsup fly

Ironclad your nerves:
should a spirit hassle the hackberry
cast it out. 20 paces or so to the cement ledge
the crumbling step that's overgrown
each yellow vine that hooks your heel
face the grove
it runs acres, acres north
clang a cast-iron skillet with a serving fork
then when a mile round
tines vibrate (the fork's and the stag's)
for the hills the stag will run—that's the spirit
hold still. the place where a fawn's nestled

Have a boy:
tinsel scotched to the screen door

Have a girl:
Adeline

Sort the cold from the feverish:
wanderlust from wandering lost
succor from suture
the cold the feverish
burn their bedclothes

Work the signs:
in the burnt-out filling station
in milk crates copperheads
a glass harmonica

players wet fingers
a blue jay nest
a kid with the fever taps a freckled shell
baby, baby, did you caw? did you caw?
Eyecandy in tongues, her apple
cheeks, her upper lip stuck to her teeth
Eyecandy's fingernails glitter and fleck off

Abbreviate:
sooner or later we all got to molt

Drive, fly, you lucky bastard—
from rose fever from milk poison
from crumps from landfills
from lagoon dumps drive
before your luck is up
before you spy yourself in the buffed chrome
of a truck up on concrete blocks

Try an opossum sequel:
simple—buy a gun

Let bygones:

Peek into outer space:
an eyeball through the treillage
your fingers through the treillage
through wormhole after wormhole

Rig your Chevy into a time machine:
copper lips copperhead tattoo stag
stiletto. Eyecandy thrusts her hips
thumbs through belt loops—1-2-1-2
2 bottles of Boone's, 1 flatbed
unzip studded jeans along the inseam
her tan line—your indian summer

Take the host:
your incisors tweeze stamen from honeysuckle

Face the ghosts:
those twin petal lobes you've unbuckled

11 a.m. Aubade

Eyecandy leaves V. Cleb's screen door open
lets every fruit fly in the county in. In jean shorts,
in an arms-tore-out sweatshirt, Eyecandy
shinnies down the mountain
past the oxeyes, the blow-up
pool, flowering satellite
dish. Past one grocery cart, 24 tulip
branches. Through a hundred *you were here* honeybees.

        V. Cleb ass-drags up, grips the particleboard TV stand.
        Through the screen, he
        blows. Hotboxes his filterless.

Eyecandy her clove. Pockets the stub.
The joint the fishers she passes pass. Who drop
one then two
dynamite bottles in
the lagoon dump. Who eye—
you sweet—the purple mouth
on the back of her neck.
Eyecandy bites her thumb
stabs it into the bottleneck of
this very
second—

Never put a chicken-shit
mayday note in a pint
of Boone's. Any drunk
fuck might save you.

        V. Cleb drunk-chicken-breakfasts at his card table.

Eyecandy kneels at an open basement
window at the head of the hollow,
her mouth an *O* against half-
strung venetian blinds.

To Blackjack Boy—shrunken arm rocking in the socket,
shrunken hand curved, the good one deals—
she hollers—*You best count V. Cleb in.*

                        Wads of Washingtons rubber-banded to his thigh, V. Cleb
                        karate kicks in his side yard. He war

                              cries—*Kiai.*

BLAM

                                                Sky high go
                        the baby fish

            swim bladders

                                      BLAM

                  Gut-deep wade

those fishers.

Eyecandy's brass hoops
the last of a lemon icebox
on a kitchenette counter

           V. Cleb kung-fu-fingers the mountain echoes—
           Likewise wiseass.

V. Cleb kung-fu-fingers the mountain
the mountain just forgets. Forgotten too—
Eyecandy's brass hoops, a lemon icebox
on the kitchenette counter. *Hush.*

Hush, baby. Yonder dynamite fishers on their backs asleep in low fog. Sh. Yonder Jack o' Lantern shrooms on a felled trunk—lights on a barge. How fishers conjure brook trout in the middle of late morning lagoon dumps.

V. Cleb cries. In his side yard, there in thin boxers, karate kicks.

Eyecandy with Blackjack Boy. Eyecandy through rusted bars painted over. Blackjack Boy—cinder block arm curls in a flooded basement, cash strapped to his thigh, spade in his chest pocket. Her lips, a smear of coral, on his dick. She slips him a slip—*You ought count V. Cleb in.*

No, she's tiptoe under a burned attic
window frame at the foot
of the hollow.
Eyecandy's mouth's no
more than a line.

A little prayer. Unstrung
behind venetian blinds,
V. Cleb makes a finger steeple

on the card table—*She put*
> *a chicken-shit mayday note in*
> *a pint of Boone's. Any*
> *drunk fuck may fuck*
> *her. Listen. Any*
> *drunk fucking fuck.*

Balancing stick in hand,
Eyecandy paces a felled trunk, almost
takes a spill. She pulls
her thumb from the bottle-
neck of this very second. Sees
all this spill out around her—fishers calling
Sooie to the purple mouth on the back of her neck, lagoon dump spilling, clover
   going yellow
              yellow
      gone.

Fishers pull one
then two dud
dynamite bottles from the lagoon dump.
One holds his breath, passes the roach. Eyecandy hotboxes
her clove. V. Cleb his filterless.

Through the screen he counts a
hundred *you don't know shit* honeybees,
an upside-down-one-
wheel-spinning grocery cart. The
countless tulip branches.

                In jean shorts, in V. Cleb's arms-
                  tore-out sweatshirt, Eyecandy
                      climbs the mountain to his oxeyes, his blow-
                          up pool, flowering satellite dish. V. Cleb
                              grips the particleboard TV stand—
                                  steady, boy—crashes back

on the floor mattress. Eyecandy leaves

                                    V. Cleb's screen door open—

Eyecandy at 15

Daydreaming is roller-skating backwards to a couples' song with a red jean banana bag—alone, not thinking—tons of lights on iodine-looking walls. Wallflower girl couples and the County Fair daisies, roses on their cheeks crack when she goes by so her banana bag spills: broken roll-on strawberry gloss, bummed bong, red twelve-toothed pocket comb, thong. *Cunty cunts! You're lucky I've got a peace sign carved into my ankle.*

•

Daydreaming they'll all turn down the rollaway cot, they'll comb the cinder block hovels, the hollow, then the mountain fog—get cut up in blackberry thickets she put a spell on—all night for her:

1) her eating the nuts off a beech
2) her eating the nuts, carpenter ants the falling beech
3) nutshells and lines of eating carpenter ants daydreamed from a hollowed-out beech
4) beech stump, Blue Dream spray-paint, redheaded woodpecker, crushed Colt
5) couldn't she just count crows—fake crows made from coat hangers and pantyhose—all day at the fog line until she falls off

•

She can get mean-feeling when she gets looked at a little long. Daydreaming is shining deer with a jacklight. Lit, shining whitetail from a truck jacked-up on concrete blocks, on tire rims and 2x4's. Freezing doe eyes with a jacklight from a chalky bed, chalk of deep woods volcanoes with a boy, or two.

•

High in a red bra and thong swimming all night in the motel swimming pool inside the padlocked chain-link that cuts into her thighs under the unlit motel swimming pool sign. Swimming pool inside the bad luck chain-link like a sky: milky clouds circling her thighs, toy airplane bumping the steps, beach ball sinking.

V. Cleb Has a Girl, Baptizes Her

Adeline in the blow-up pool
lays her here in the side yard
half-born
(she made a quarter hour)
under a half-step headstone
by half a sedan
(transmission greasing the hood)

couple Washingtons slid in
a flour sack she just fits in
banjo-faced and the crown
a see-through
blue through burlap

Swears he'll hear
his girl grow:
a seventeen-year locust molting
for the last time

V. Cleb, hears himself say,
a Mason jar, a bar of
lye on the sill—
*no point making yourself good
looking no more.*
                      You ain't hearing

*me, God. My flesh
and what else washed down
with the shave water?*

His Bed Sheet in Place

of a door. Behind it Eyecandy
in place of a wife, her water

broke and the junk on his hands
his hands in place of Doc-boy's
his hands scratching round for ammonia
place of smelling salts
red purse in place of a medicine bag
hands tugging at a blue mute
place of a baby, named for a country tune
place of a hymn, washing its body
a blow-up pool in place of a tub
place of a baptismal font
place of living water

Thought it'd be easy to act like other folks
Is it easy

Primer from His Forebears

augur like us

bloodlet

cure indian tobacco
and whooping cough

ditch homemade silencers

fiddle *pretty Red Wing*
weeping her heart away

hang a full-length hog
like Pa Bud

heist getaway skiffs

idle in mountain laurel

know hognose
from timber rattler

load polkstaff muskets

name the preacher
like Mary Jane
there's the SOB got me pregnant

paddle Snake Mountain
arms for oars

read stars with it

tie brake-logs to wagons

barn-raise like us

bootleg

down lame curs
and indian tonic

egress highland
for highland

girdle trees
like Nan Moon

heist headstones

idle like us

jaybird in mountain streams
longer still

lump it winters
off squirrel, flies, lobelia

marry up like Beersheeba

own your bastards
like nary a one
I'm the SOB got her pregnant

quote your *Farmer's Almanac*

salt another clan's still

use leftovers you land

vie for local girls

whitewash camp houses

yen like us

zero your sights

war like Overmountain Men

X your name like Big Go-Go
and her ilk

zero like us

zero your odometer
before you enter

Instrument Control Panels

Raven Spell

shaggy-throat!
shit-eater!
old ballyhoo!

black
the head-
lights, bank
this chevy
hull its

dog pens
dovecotes
milk crates

where lie down
blue tick
with bobcat
also grouse
with dove

drown
in rain-
bow oil
plumage

hinterland
my bones

stomping ground
my ribcage

stone's throw
my brains

my skull
for barbed
wire nests

to glister
opened window
to pass

be fledgling
be scripture
be bluebottle

fly

Necrology from His Forebears

Cirrhosis. Childbirth. Sugar. Old age, plain and simple.

In state asylums. In homemade stills peeling grapes. In lousy two-foot streams. In a pool of blood round Mattie shucking peas.

Shotgun wound. Self-inflicted
to the back of the head.
So they say.
That was Neartye Agile.

Henpeck set into blood poison—John Frederick around the time his wife quickened.

Measles fever at three, at six, at sixteen.

In a hospital bed. Your daddy. Opened up bedside, as they say. His breastbone broken. On purpose. Fearing it readying to come through. Shard and splinter of it. Through his great gray chest curls.

Scrap of a shape note hymn heard in passing.
Through *horizon adorning*
honey locusts.
By first light.

The pear tree a flock of turkeys about stripped.
Under it
Mary Jane went,
Meet my maker when I goddamn well feel like it.

On a two-way mountain pass just outside White County, Tennessee. Bushwhacked on a wagon of pilfered corn. Lorenzo Ting. Soaking his baby's bonnet and asking the killers, *My baby?* Faceup he was found.

Asking the timberline. Asking the warble.

Lived seventy-six more years, Ting's baby did.
Went in the bed she was born in.
Peaceful in her sleep, as they say.

This is what she said when you were born—
This one here acts like he been here before.

Mama Cleb Took Up Her Homemade Torch

left the wash
the washbasin's veiny porcelain

for the Word
                         Who's inviolate?
                                      A-men
                    Who'd not cut the rings off their dead?

Mama Cleb's ringless
ring finger inside the kerosene
flame   Antenna
in a chinaberry

                        Who is it who's not first born dead?
                                Alleluia A-men

Afire

Why, Mama Cleb
prayed, *Why the roup*
took my half dozen handfed birds

Inside the washbasin
                       underclothes
Inside Mama Cleb
                       her firstborn

Mama Cleb's veiny hand passed whole through the flame

Idolize her
way back when
                       her crystal set

Her radio preacher   (530 kHz)
                               False idols, you hear?

Idolize Tennessee
                      Ernie Ford
                      (860 kHz)

                      You load sixteen tons, what do you get?
                      The neighbor's barn-
                          raising bonfire mail-order guitars   cloggers

Idolize Mama Cleb's Grand Opry
under the chinaberry's oxygen
tent in the homestead

                      V. Cleb was getting named under

                      hay   moon   thunder

                    moon   mead   full buck   moon

                                                                       Vitalis
                                    Vitalis
                    Vitalis

V. Cleb at 8

A primordial mountain. Daybreak.

Cue the smoke-edged cowboy
boulders backdrop

Out of yellow smoke
                                    a ten-gallon tenor on the catwalk
                                    catwalk of fly-rock steppingstones
who knows how to fuck with the future

Some opera this—a boy in the pit
of a gorge, a boy and a burlap
                                    of blind cats in the pit of a gorge
                                    ruffed grouse, cottonmouth
cues the ovenbird overture then the

    BLIND CAT CHORUS:
    If you untie this burlap, Vitalis

                Mama Cleb shall appear

                                under a sapling
                                just here she's
                                toking a joint
                                cheek-to-cheek
                                in joined sleeping bags
                                with the ten-gallon tenor

    MAMA CLEB ARIA:
    A starlet silk
    trilling moss
    cold rocks

MAMA CLEB AND TEN-GALLON TENOR DUET:
  If you do not untie the burlap
     if you do not put your hand in
         we will go back into our yellow smoke
              the yellow smoke into the smoke-edged cowboy boulders
                  smoke-edged cowboy boulders
                                      into tree-
                                      shaped
                                      clouds

                    and the blind cats
                    will burrow
                    the creek

long vowels up from its slimy arrowhead mouth-to-mouth bottom

                                          the creek
                                        will rise

To Heavy Metal from a Boom Box

the little ass-kicker
out of pit dust
a hero rises—
feathers black
glazed red
glazed black so tonight you
can't even
tell birds apart—
all combs and wattles cut,
spurs filed,
gashes or sutures where
feathers won't grow,
mouths boys suck blood
out of, spit, blow in,
rub the feathers like any fur,
untape razors,
wager, take the living into
the pit by their feet,
prop them up, touch
beak to beak—
tip-
toe,
they hulk,
cannot cut,
doped on
gunpowder.
Hackles sunray.
One slips onto its back,
neck curved up,
head erect.
Guts out,
the other hovers,
a leg down,
dive-bombs the one underneath.
The little ass-kicker rises, asks what
to worship—

No Jukebox, No Payphone

no slot machine, but a motel bed
he puts his coin in

Eyecandy mashed against the headboard—
the maple veneer nearly picked off
a pillow under the small of her back
pillow pattern over her face

Is there a pattern to the bottle rings
old and new, on the nightstand?
Was Adeline mine?

Her cigarette butts swell, they float
Don't take scrip, V. Cleb, no,
this mattress vibrates for a quarter
and for a nickel bag I'll—shrugs

The screen's stapled shut. No bugs,
deer spray, but other things lurk
here. Others need fixing—
a bottle behind the busted TV screen's claw
the shaggy nails behind her press-ons

Beyond this shit-colored curtain
headlights, lounger straps, chain-link
slash up blacktop, drained pool, door 57

Here is the nightstand, Gideon's inside

Parable from His Forebears

During the Easter homily, the Holiness preacher used the phrase *slain in the Spirit* twenty some odd times. And spent his pauses three ways: exhaling *ha*, touching the death certificate—his own, a snakebite—in his breast pocket, drinking from a half-gallon canning jar of strychnine. Other times the keyboard or drums added a flourish.

Too cold—must have been—to gather copperheads or rattlers from Gum Fork: no serpent boxes at the altar. No propane torches.

The sermon was about clearing a neighbor's land. When they were pulling back the canebrake, they found an old corncrib and under some boards a store of—paused here, took a huge swig—home canned peaches sixty years old. Some shrugged relief, and some were let down it wasn't pelf.

One woman skipped through the aisles throughout the service. He put on a woman's voice then: *Don't you eat them. It'll poison you.*

Which is true. Eventually. Botulism, some such. Days before it kicks in sometimes. Gut rot. Paralysis.

Some danced in the aisles with one hand up testifying and like a pole was up their backs. So they ate them all, the land clearers the peaches, and they were the best tasting peaches anybody had ever had.

And then one very old woman, the only in gingham, went up front and we all laid hands on her. The circle migrated but stayed up front and made low sounds. While the boy—couldn't have been more than ten—played drums and the preacher started us singing, *I'm Going On*. Did we mean *Home?*

Warning Lights and Gauges

Fable from His Forebears

Some folks don't believe in birds. A big old black bird landed right there dropping its wing down off our roof. Right down the center of the house. Sure enough, that's where we found my dog dug out under the kitchen. Ate the gray poison toad—chasing it since he was a pup. Dragged him out by the scruff. A far piece from the house. Went right-handed at the road down to where the culvert gets shrubby. Covers him up. And that old black bird turned to watch us. Then took off. Back, like as not, from whence it came. Some folks don't believe in birds. *Crow buzzard. Buzzard vulture. Vulture raven. Raven.* Call them what you will, you ought believe in birds. If you want to be let alone. Otherwise, they'll perch to warn you. If you take no heed, they'll pluck your roof. Pluck the thatch till the mountain dumps snow on your bed. Wake up. Thank the bird. *Thanks for letting on there's a boneyard under my feet.*

Poison's Out

so's shit that
goes round
in pairs:
snakes, girls
and *look up!*
the
Twins

AM's on
and sludge in
side yards
rising
Newsflash
it ain't oil
it ain't the devil
pissing on his ceiling

Looked at's
looking back
Hood drinker
Stargazer
Delta Dawn
Delta Dawn
What's that
What's that flower
What wrong
thing's always taking
V. Cleb's poison
covering its tracks

Yonder jaw
upon jaw
every last
trap rusted
rusted the
fuck open

The Holy Ghost Might Appear

as Bruce Lee's

hanging his nunchuks

round V. Cleb's neck

like a spirit-

filled handler

a rattler

What Place Then for a Creator?

The dead girl decks herself in redbud, red algae, red-shouldered hawk for Cleb

She swims through reeds to his sick room

She burns sassafras in the mountain cave

She steeps black elder tea

She reads *is smoke is smoke is smoke*

She hangs gourds in a chinaberry

She hangs chinaberry and owl in eventide

She charms him with water moccasins

She charms them from water from skins from cans of lard

She puts her fingers and tongue through a treillage of green heron horse nettle

She molds double vowels to her gums—*sweet gum woolly adelgid*

She speaks through fever dreams in tongues without skulls

She is like the blood thrown from his window

She greens his sunken chassis in splendor

        o earthen vessel   o living water   o algaeic angel

The Burnt-out Filling Station

where he used to take up rattlers
a little gal the age Adeline would be
(were she)
in maybe her brother's swim trunks
in maybe her daddy's hawaiian shirt
hand squeezing a note
this time
you be dead
wood for me
to bloom on
ponytail dripping
bones sticking out
visor bending the sun

Inspector in His Mint Suit

filling an ink pen on the half-step, saying there's "Radio Action"
in V. Cleb's well. Saying, *You ain't well*
                                      and mutes some twenty gadgets

Here's the static V. Cleb's fluent in: his finger in an electric
socket until Jesusbaby comes,
                          other things that break up:

purple florets and fur of his last sweet potato
Of his last bowl of coffee
                          did he boil out the lead?

Is there lead in Adeline? Her rabbit hole. Her black-eyed Susans
Her plastic tulips—
                  the inspector's empty buttonhole—

Ghosts

still others he can see through—
        the caul he's born with
        the sheet he's dead under
        the louse on his thigh
        the gold paint on Eyecandy's face
        the tie strings on her nightie, her nightie
        the lamp on the nightstand
        a night lizard on the stapled screen, the screen
        and his front teeth
        and Adeline

Is there a bottom to the muddy lagoon he used to lap?

Quantum Mechanical Eyecandy

Lagoon bottom
where her wound widens and fingerprints unfurl—
the eyelids long gone.

Whether blade or purloined pearl handle
buried in bramble
near her depends on who is looking.

A red-headed woodpecker goes *jotjot jotjotjotjot*
A different take—

her absence branches with the white pine
that blisters
like her shoulders

in full sun
and she's on the bank on her belly, oiled up,
straps down,

eyes closed,
thinking how it's better to be seen than sighted,

than take in
every eyesore in this mountain head hollow

that won't glue together even when looked at,
jotjotjot
that sounds when listened for. Bird

and no bird, trunk hole
and trunk whole,

sunbather bathed, at once, in shade and water.
In water her body moves like, moved by
something alive—

itsy square by itsy square she's preyed upon by
prey she hides.
Old tan lines blur, her skin branches lightly.

jotjotjot—Freezes a fawn in fauna, mouthful of clover.

Sh of a footprint
through leaf-like leaves. The green shoots won't tell—

(soft mouth
softer clover)

Devil Worshipers Say It

with us   Float off
      Float off
little tie-on
little tie-on
nightie thing
nightie thing
like fuzz
like fuzz
off a window unit
off a window unit
and tie up
and tie up
the tongues
the tongues
she's speaking in
she's speaking in
Adeline was maybe mine
Adeline was maybe mine
     float off
float off
lye soap that gave me
lies hope that gave me
the albino eye
        the elbowed eye
float louse float louse off you
darting through
my pubes
no, float off chicken knife
with the melted handle that I pin now like
a dart to her throat
float
off messy mattress and the shag carpet
say who
    her   who

her
who gizzard-mess is
seeping through

Didn't go right
Float

Roadside Emergencies

Sears Catalog Girl Grants V. Cleb the Spiritual Gifts of Flight and X-ray Vision

In white-stitch Holy Ghost spirit jeans
in an Outer Space revelation vest
stitched with twelve quarter-size mirrors she steps off
the half color half page ad
into the passenger seat
where the triple shag floorboard tries to drown her ankle
boots her thighs
where by the dome bulb by the AM dial
by the Chevy headlight off the lagoon dump
Sears Catalog Girl undoes her silver-turning-
green Leaf & Vine
belt to reveal—
not some copperhead gut tattoo—
rings of shingle blisters
she half moans
her head half turned on the seam-busted headrest: *Ain't we all hiding
some kind of plague under our fig leaf, Vitalis Cleb?*

•

Ain't we all hiding some kind under our fig leaf?
Sears Girl takes the nail-bat
from the deer-hooves-hot-glued-hound-fur gun rack
swoops it round the cab

Those two sixty-penny nails they ache to be wings

                      this nail-bat—a biplane—

                                        it lifts

from this achy lagoon dump lifts this dynamite-bottle-shard achy this
sliced-underpants-rusted-to-the-last-flatbed-in-this-hollow achy lagoon dump lifts

low flies   over the strip   mined drag strip over the cut down still

       over the two-necked cotton gin

                So long peeling sedan top
                So long bleach-cut shine
                So long brown lung
                So long   you hear

•

Hear the biplane fog-hover
over a brush arbor revival
paper plates fatback potted meat
Dixie cups and bit-up fingers and finger nubs
Brush arbor revival
V. Cleb—foggy
hair swirling black
jeans muscling—on the sea-
sick barge of a picnic table
preaches backed by branchy mountains

Here fog is the mist turning
in a pint of lye hid in the slatted pit
viper box it hinges
on V. Cleb's digital wristwatch

•

    V. Cleb fogs then sets the digital watch face—

       Here fog's a tinted arcade front

       It begs you—*Believe without sight*
       in a headbanger: his tits and crossbones T-shirt

his fingers in Sears Catalog Girl her jeans
teenage tongue along her double teeth

her hitched up on an outer space
video game

                      A coin slot
                      owns this hollow's night-
                      life: its blast
                      furnace flares
                      its brush arbor blessings
                      its passion
                      leopard-printing
                      backseats
                      front porch settees
                      Night is an umbrella
                      duct taped
                      to a baby stroller

Fog a tinted arcade front
From spaceship
through starry
video screen
Sears Catalog Girl's moany head:
Why's it all an iron-on decal to you, Vitalis?
Kicking off bobby socks boots she calls:
Can you believe
in the snake bites
on my ankle bones?

                      •

Can you believe in the snake bites on my ankle bones?
Can you in the brush arbor of salvation cocktails?

        Sock feet tread pit vipers
        Hands blot burning faces with toilet paper
                      salve with soda water

while still
unforgiveness piggybacks
V. Cleb

while still he preaches and paces the picnic table

as fog goes up

           branchy mountains

                        and the table's feet
                                      disappear
                                          in
                                          earth

Somebody pass this on:
Fog's a barghest's paw print
you hunt it   it you
bum flashlight
dirt
yard

           Day a mirrored pinwheel turns
           the torch cut trailer-shack

           your dirt yard
           lambent sheet metal porch
           V. Cleb arms crossed

           under his wife-beater at 11 a.m.
           fevers like a musical saw
           sixer dazzling

           in the cushionless hollow
           of a flowery settee

Ain't we all hiding some kind of plague under our fig leaf, Vitalis? she whistles across open beers

closes and then heals
his albino eye

    He testifies:

> *I see this outdoor living room*
> *I see this fish knife this fish kettle*
> *I see inside the tied out hound*
>
>   *I see vocal cords I slice*
>
> *I see inside the sun-bleached reindeer laid on a sawhorse*
>
> *See it think:*
> Woe let me grow back my red lips Vitalis
> O woe let me grow back my white spots too Vitalis

Morning blow-up pool see you tomorrow
washing down the mountain stuck with pine needles
Hey rocking three-legged
swing set—rusty mouth-
holes all over you—you give me
Adeline's ghost swinging—a pink froth hat on her water-head
Give me Adeline's ghost—a pink froth hat blowing off

    As the leaky snipe hunting bag softens the yellow porch wood
    as yellow shimmies up the legs of the flowery settee
    up V. Cleb's pocked-up shins

                        he gives a mind-reading wink
        to the criss-cross door window
        and in this shaft he does a last eagle claw he yawns

and the biplane tilts to fit through the torch cut trailer-shack window

                                      of V. Cleb's

                                            mouth

•

Of V. Cleb's mouth
                    Thrush-mottled entrance
Tinsel strung doorframe
                    Flooded carpet's burns
Ache of hog skins in dripping lye
                    Drop of boneset tea on bone china
Stick-on cross: the center a silver-pink Jesusbaby, silver its posies

                    Never thinking you'd go
Bermuda triangle in that Catalog Girl,
                    rubbing the onion
skin, rubbing her thigh neck tit till
                    that hot gal is a night
air sieve you fall through
                    Why's everybody else's hard-on
a homing pigeon?

                    Pulley bone on bone china
Lone bar of Octagon Soap on the sill
                    Orange wing bars of a thrush it is a pupil
in your square of kitchen light
                    Pines backlit orange through plexiglas

Do the glass test on your baby's rash

        Make your kitchen sink an ice bath

The white-blue ripples like the ripples of Baby Vitalis' feverish thighs

        One worldwide shower curtain

between the pantry and the icebox and the sink of iced

        fish heads Having had plain faith

there was somebody on the other side

        Having had homemade TV dinners

Having had three-handed bridge

        Having saucer-drunk jerk coffee

And chugged straight Little Bo Peep

        Having had highs Sears Girl could wrap her blotchy labile

thighs round—

> *Ain't we all hiding*
> *ain't we all*
> *somebody's plague*
> *somebody else under*
> *our fig leaf?*

        •

        We see the pit viper nostrils
        of your windpipe V. Cleb

        Don't you want...

    Jerk the curtain off its rings stop
    the watch face open
    the peach can

        See yourself foggy and nostriled in the lid
           See yourself in the chicken knife

    Fish gig
    this holy peach

Is there no holy peach?
See yourself see
the bedroom in your gut Vitalis Cleb

Is there no bedroom in your gut?
No Mama Cleb
yellow slip bone stave corset
cough drop between her double teeth
        —remember—
on the mattress edge it matches her thighs?

No Little Boy Vitalis
seen through the bedroom window
pacing an ark no ark
hand built in the dirt yard
hand in hand with her
boy aftereyes snake and earthworm:
Look over look Mama Cleb at all that

    We see you Boy Vitalis   no not catsup-covered
                                            opened by the electric cutter

   —there there—

held together by her girdle

    See you yes   half on the mattress

        feet cocked on a dresser

                          There's Eyecandy spread-eagle
                          in a knotted little girl T-shirt

                                        knocked up, fleshy
                                        runs in blue underpants
                                        hickey on a spine
                                        huffing paint in a world
                                        famous Chevy bed

There Adeline her head a pink balloon in the blow-up pool

There Eyecandy frying in baby oil in the bed a mountain ash is blowing over her

        Asks, *Is there no room in your gutted bed?*

        We see the bedroom in your gut, Vitalis Cleb

There plastic framed flowers *pink pink pink* on blue cork

        See a yellow-filmed supper
            on the devotion booklet
            on the prayer cloth
            on the TV set

a water
streaked gold
checkered lamp
on a swirled amber dresser
with a mirrorless handheld
that would show
the ceiling Mama Cleb would see
prostrate a rag not over her face

        where you weep and nuzzle her chest
        —I know—
        the vegetable dye grown out
        so white roots fan round her face

    Nothing so light as the halo round a fast-eating gut cancer

Ain't we
all somebody else?
Sears Catalog Girl lifts the rag
off Mama Cleb's face

Watch her lips:
>   *Can you gather pit vipers with a hook cane*
>   *in a mountain*
>   *in winter?*

Customer Assistance

Did the Universe Have a Beginning, and If So, What Happened Before Then?

Then. It took
off. An ark
was the ribcage
of a horse a
dog drags and gnaws
and drags past
a world of curs
left behind.
An afterlife
was the costume
of a blue jay.
Cleb, I found it.
Now. Put it on.
This. This. This.

What Is It That Breathes Fire into the Equation and Makes a Universe to Destroy?

Dear paint huffers

Dear drummers of knees, of paint cans, of air

Dear lagoon and, yes, dirty dances to Walkmans and, yes, I am 16 and moonwalking lagoons

Dear rags, rags in mouths

Dear airwaves of Aerosmith's *Backstroke lover always hidin' 'neath the covers*

Dear paint huffers lagoonside

Dear kisses blown to aerodynamic bods, silver mouths, aortic breaststrokes like this

Dear ankles and dandelion anklets

Dear neck rubs Dear longnecks Dear King Cobras

Dear pinkie nail that feathers Eyecandy's knee, runs inside my bikini elastic

Dear boy's pinkie nail that susurrates, *coke or guitar pick?*
                                                      susurrates
                                                      inside me

Dear paint huffers huffing silver lagoonside
                your languish
                                your language
                                                  12-gauge

            Lagoon
                                thy oldness
                                                  thy wholeness

thy black hole
Eyecandy
    you tough, tough girl

        lipstick black   mood ring   shank

    i. My mood ring a catfish smelling with its whole body
    ii. My lipstick a merle crashing through your kitchen window
    iii. My shank, ladies, in the school gym locker

O Eyecandy, what if time is this chain I wormhole through, in silver nostril, out zitty mouth, time the plastic paint bag we balloon

    Dear Paleolithicandy what if I'm surrounding
                          what if I'm surrounding
                                            what if
                                          I'm sur-
                              rounding
                  this
        lagoon

O paint huffer lover, Eyecandy will relive you ripping your good button-down like you didn't care again on the gymnasium dance floor I'm breathing fire

O what if time is a pinstripe you're spinning
                                            barely   promise me

each button'll fly
Fell

Did the Universe Have a Beginning, and If So, What Happened Before Then?

When the brightest aurora borealis ever known in this county arose, people could be heard praying in almost every part of the neighborhood

Kettles in the open and grape arbors splitting under blackberry tonnage

What's given way to

Names for dwelling in—Bon Air Springs, Ravenscroft, Sunset Rock

My grandmother's pinning bills to her underthings, but I always thought who knows when a feeling-up might happen

She made her sundowns of oat straw. Barefoot for church

Of course, mattresses, safes, and trunks

As one settler said to his spilled drink, "Oh, yes; I know you're good but I can't get to you"

Names you could pass through on—Roane County, Calfkiller River

After I would flatten my hand hard for the medium-colored horse to eat her sugar cubes, I was thought a girly-girl

Ought to count herself lucky. First in the family to keep her teeth this long

You mean to tell me a perfectly normal 25-year-old man died of a henpeck. Set into blood poisoning. You mean sepsis. Why'd they call him Fred if his name was John

What might become a setting

Each rooster to its tether

Family or no, didn't that son of a bitch say I made his mashed potatoes soapy

Everybody had the good sense to steer clear of the Two-Seed-in-the-Spirit revival tents. Though I liked to listen outside

How can I know where a thing is but not my damn self

Even the birds and things it will have dawned on when all around

mountains
wash away
mountains
wash away
mountains

Why Do We Remember the Past and Not the Future?

A woman from Arkansas calls into a talk show to tell how she got up in the middle of Sunday dinner, literally dropping the cornbread from her mouth—*choking*, her husband and kids must have thought—then told the table, "Something has happened to my mother." Then the rest home in California called. On his way home, my father felt his father beside him in the Taurus. Then felt him get out at the light by Red Lobster the moment my grandfather died in Texas. My cousin, the age then I am now, running drugs from the city park, ran his motorcycle 80 mph into a tree on a country road, White County, Tennessee. In Bristol, my grandmother saw him at her bedroom window, "Granny, let me in."

    Remember a neighbor girl stung near to death

Isopentyl acetate, alarm pheromone, also called banana or pear oil, released by the honeybee when it stings. Lures the others out of hives, out of roses, out of standing ponds.

Find a fast-running spring, dunk your head under. Those bees'll wait though. On the banks. Wait. Wait hours for you.

    Remember that neighbor girl stung near to death
                  Remember her eyebrows, hair will never grow back

    A girl, I wrote, I'd name for a country tune

    Memorize that: A girl I'd call

                              Sweet Adeline, sweet Adeline

                                    My Adeline, my Adeline
You're the flower of my…flower of my…something, something, something… *For you I pine.* Remember my childhood house (cedar-shake) and the woods the "hillbilly hippies" lived in, their tents *down by the brook-side. To find all vanished,* chestnut blight of the 30s, butternut *I wonder where you are* canker, dogwood anthracnose, *dream gone by* beech scales going whole hog for the bark *in the sighing wind. Sweet Adeline,* old fashioned, Old German name,

mountain song, *flower of my*...

    Elms, I smell your old mold

            Earth   your mud-huts cracking

                    Fence   your electric

                                Traps   your night crawlers crawling

    Outdoor steps, I memorize your carpet

        Snow   your cottonmouth

            Raccoon   your dropped tail

Memorize *opossum*—the long, longing vowel dropped centuries back except by us highlanders. Variegated pinks of its beak flash. Open. Opossum the size of a cat in the cat food.

        Memorize this coyote will rise from a badger hole
  Rise from a badger hole to drink from the lagoon

                      •

Morning, tent city. Morning, dirtbag hippies on dirt bikes. You can't hear me. Morning, dirt-poor orange lilies that ain't lilies.

    Among them remember the past and the future

        Call the opossum, milk carton in hand, like a cat
        Here thing

Learn the blue heeler to heel with a hickory branch. Learning's a streaky chest memorizing the bark scalene.

Number of concentric circles raked in a dirt yard
　　　　　Number of ghost lights circling raked circles

Have you spied a past life or two of mine circle there

・

May 20, 1901. Truss Bridge Fails. Steam Locomotive Falls In Red River Of The South. My great-grandfather on my father's side escaped through a sleeper window, which cut his legs to the bone. His wife, Ada, talked army doctors out of transfemoral amputation. Who knew what the fuck they were doing back then. They'd hack off anything—1958, the minute cancer spread from her breasts to her spine, they cut the nerves to my mother's grandmother's legs. Ada, so I'm told, took him to Oklahoma and dressed the wound. They had iodine, they had gauze, they had Johnson & Johnson. She saved both legs.

Imagine though phantoms with phantom limbs. Rare earth magnets more than likely cure the sensation. Discover a 100,000-year-old bloodstone and magnetite mine natives used for ailments.

　　　　Phantom limb in this deep mine

　Magnets in the brains of birds hardwired to flock South
　　　　　　　To fly wouldn't you will your free will away

1953. They would sew the Metzenbaum scissors inside a polycystic great-aunt by marriage.

Did my great-grandfather, in the River, remember before he was born, remember his body hid in a cloud?

　Me I keep thinking of how I will be before all this

　　Phantom limb in this deep mine

　　　　　Heatstroke of fallen arches, of my veins collapsed
　　　　　Heatstroke of rotting fruit the sink pukes back

Children's limbs grow faster in the spring, I've read. Something I couldn't put my finger on then—endless, speeding numbers I heard inside the wee endless.

"A genetic mechanism implicates chromosome 11 in schizophrenia disease," I read they've found the breakpoint. Proof. 1st and 3rd degree relatives *(great-uncle, great-uncle, first cousin, first cousin, mother)* place me at a 19% risk. My father woke me in the middle of the night to say my cousin had "killed himself." Even though his vehicle (plus loaded operator) was only figuratively a "loaded gun," my cousin had "killed himself" for real. But figuratively he had not, you know, his will wasn't in it. So my father, knowing how it would be heard, was wrong to say it. Is dead wrong.

      Phantom limb in this deep mine

Why Does the Universe Go through the Bother of Existing?

Adeline, remember my vision of crossing, your hand in mine, the Bristol crosswalk bus exhaust. Exhaust getting in the way of clouds so I can't tell them apart. It would pour later. My Adeline, child I could, can, will, should... *How does one put it?* In all fairness I should bear in mind never bear.

    Go and see, though, is there a basket among the reeds of this lagoon bank

Bone shard in the blown-open mine

        Barn owl in the blown-open barn

                Bone owl in the blown-open open

Notes

(3) Flo—an arrow

(14) Overmountain Men—soldiers from North Carolina, Tennessee, and Virginia who defeated the British in the Battle of Kings Mountain on October 7, 1780

(36, 57, 58, 60, 62, 66) The question titles come from Hawking's documentary *A Brief History of Time*.

(48) Barghest—"goblin dog"

(51) Jerk coffee—prepared by steeping coffee beans in boiling water; the beans are quickly "jerked" out of the water to be reused

(52) Aftereye—to look after

(60) The following come from Reverend Monroe Seals' 1935 book, *History of White County:*

> "When the brightest aurora borealis ever known in this County arose, people could be heard praying in almost every part of the neighborhood."

> "She made her sundowns of oat straw."

> "As one settler said to his spilled drink, 'Oh, yes; I know you're good but I can't get to you.'"

(65) "A Genetic Mechanism Implicates Chromosome 11 in Schizophrenia and Bipolar Diseases" is the title of Amar J.S. Klar's article, which appeared in the journal *Genetics* in 2004.

Acknowledgments

Various incarnations of the poems first appeared in the following publications:

American Letters & Commentary: "To Heavy Metal from a Boom Box"

Bateau: "Quantum Mechanical Eyecandy"

burntdistrict: "What Place Then for a Creator?"

Colorado Review: "Kill the Harbinger"

DIAGRAM: "Did the Universe Have a Beginning, and If So, What Happened Before Then?" (first version) and "Fable from His Forebears"

Drunken Boat: "Primer from His Forebears"

EOAGH: "Raven Spell" and "Parable from His Forebears"

Fourteen Hills: "What Is It That Breathes Fire into the Equation and Makes a Universe to Destroy?"

Horse Less Review: "Sears Catalog Girl Grants V. Cleb the Spiritual Gifts of Flight and X-ray Vision"

Indiana Review: "V. Cleb Has a Girl, Baptizes Her," "His Bed Sheet in Place," "No Jukebox, No Payphone," "Poison's Out," "The Burnt-out Filling Station," "Inspector in His Mint Suit," "Ghosts," and "Devil Worshipers Say It"

The Journal: "Necrology from His Forebears"

New Delta Review: "V. Cleb at 8"

Ostrich Review: "Why Does the Universe Go through the Bother of Existing?"

Sonora Review: "Mama Cleb Took Up Her Homemade Torch," "Why Do We Remember the Past and Not the Future?" and "Why Does the Universe Go through the Bother of Existing?"

Sundog Lit: "Did the Universe Have a Beginning, and If So, What Happened Before Then?" (second version)

Witness: "11 a.m. Aubade" and "Eyecandy at Fifteen"

"Kill the Harbinger" was reprinted in *The Southern Poetry Anthology, Volume IV: Louisiana* (Texas Review Press, 2011).

"Fable from His Forebears," "Kill the Harbinger," and "What Is It That Breathes Fire into the Equation and Makes a Universe to Destroy?" in *Hick Poetics* (Lost Roads Press, 2015).

A portion of this work was published in the chapbook *Fever Dreams in Tongues without Skulls* (Nous-zōt Press, 2015).

My wholehearted gratitude goes to the 2015 Trio Award judge, Neil Shepard, and the Trio House Press editors, especially Tayve Neese who steadfastly and compassionately looked after this book from initial edits to final print.

Thanks to the 2015 Rochelle Ratner Award judge, Stephanie Strickland, and Marsh Hawk publisher Sandy McIntosh. Thanks to the Louisiana Division of the Arts and the University of New Orleans English Department for their generous support. I am also grateful to the staff of the Archives of Appalachia for their assistance.

Ongoing appreciation to my readers: Peter Cooley, Kay Murphy, Andy Young, Melissa Dickey, Tonya Foster, David McMahon, Laura Mullen, Marthe Reed, Ed Skoog, Abraham Smith, Andy Stallings, Shelly Taylor, Joseph P. Wood, Emily Wright, and the late Jake Adam York. I am particularly indebted to Brad Richard and Michael Tod Edgerton who critiqued several manuscript drafts of this book.

I thank the late Martha Ruth Ricks Bond, my guide back through the ancestral hills; Jonathan Padgett, my companion; Mamie 3, my spiritual gift; and the forebears (from a lap baby, listening).

About the Author

Carolyn Hembree was born in Bristol, Tennessee. Her debut poetry collection, *Skinny,* came out from Kore Press in 2012. Nous-zōt Press published her chapbook in 2015. Her work has appeared in *Colorado Review, Drunken Boat, The Journal, Poetry Daily,* and other publications. She is the recipient of the 2015 Marsh Hawk Press Rochelle Ratner Prize, selected by Stephanie Strickland. She has received grants and fellowships from PEN, the Louisiana Division of the Arts, and the Southern Arts Federation. An assistant professor at the University of New Orleans, Carolyn teaches writing and serves as poetry editor of *Bayou Magazine.*

About the Book

Rigging a Chevy into a Time Machine and Other Ways to Escape a Plague was designed at Trio House Press through the collaboration of:

Tayve Neese, Lead Editor
Dorinda Wegener, Cover Design
Lea Deschenes, Interior Design

The text is set in Adobe Caslon Pro.

The publication of this book is made possible, whole or in part, by the generous support of the following individuals and/or agencies:

Anonymous

About the Press

Trio House Press is a collective press. Individuals within our organization come together and are motivated by the primary shared goal of publishing distinct American voices in poetry. All THP published poets must agree to serve as Collective Members of the Trio House Press for twenty-four months after publication in order to assist with the press and bring more Trio books into print. Award winners and published poets must serve on one of four committees: Production and Design, Distribution and Sales, Educational Development, or Fundraising and Marketing. Our Collective Members reside in cities from New York to San Francisco.

Trio House Press adheres to and supports all ethical standards and guidelines outlined by the CLMP.

The Editors of Trio House Press would like to thank Neil Shepard.

Trio House Press, Inc. is dedicated to the promotion of poetry as literary art, which enhances the human experience and its culture. We contribute in an innovative and distinct way to American Poetry by publishing emerging and established poets, providing educational materials, and fostering the artistic process of writing poetry. For further information, or to consider making a donation to Trio House Press, please visit us online at: www.triohousepress.org.

Other Trio House Press Books you might enjoy:

Bone Music by Stephen Cramer
    2015 Louise Bogan Award selected by Kimiko Hahn

Magpies in the Valley of Oleanders by Kyle McCord, 2015

Your Immaculate Heart by Annmarie O'Connell, 2015

The Alchemy of My Mortal Form by Sandy Longhorn
    2014 Louise Bogan Winner selected by Carol Frost

What the Night Numbered by Bradford Tice
    2014 Trio Award Winner selected by Peter Campion

Flight of August by Lawrence Eby
    2013 Louise Bogan Winner selected by Joan Houlihan

The Consolations by John W. Evans
    2013 Trio Award Winner selected by Mihaela Moscaliuc

Fellow Odd Fellow by Steven Riel, 2013

Clay by David Groff
    2012 Louise Bogan Winner selected by Michael Waters

Gold Passage by Iris Jamahl Dunkle
    2012 Trio Award Winner selected by Ross Gay

If You're Lucky Is a Theory of Mine by Matt Mauch, 2012

www.ingramcontent.com/pod-product-compliance
Lightning Source LLC
Chambersburg PA
CBHW020622300426
44113CB00007B/751